CHEF IN A JAR

CEC Horace Callwood
Chef in a Jar

Published by Spines
ISBN: 979-8-89691-935-3

CHEF IN A JAR

MENUS AND RECIPES

CEC HORACE CALLWOOD

CONTENTS

ABOUT THE AUTHOR

Horace Callwood is a 69-year-old retired certified executive chef and owner/operator who was responsible for day-to-day operations. His duties included purchasing, budgeting, record management, payroll, and quality assurance. He closely monitored employees, interacted with customers, and managed all human resources aspects, including recruiting, selection, training, scheduling, and supervision. He also monitored food waste.

Professional Experience:

- **2000 - 2006:** Tony and Joe's Seafood Place, Washington, DC

Position: Executive Chef

- Managed a staff of 45 exempt and non-exempt employees while developing and maintaining a diverse, cross-trained core staff in a seasonal operation.

- Reduced food costs to the restaurant's record low while improving food quality.

• **1989 - 1990:** Virgin Isle Hotel, St. Thomas, U.S. Virgin Islands

Position: Executive Chef

- Managed a staff of 35 union employees, enhancing relations between management and the bargaining unit.

- Oversaw three kitchens, two dining rooms, and three large banquet halls.

- Achieved record-low food and labor costs while improving food quality.

• **2000:** American Culinary Federation

- Completed certification as an Executive Chef.

• **1988:** Culinary School of Washington, DC

- Completed the Chef's training program and designed plate presentations.

- Somewhere between 1988 and 1989, the U.S. Virgin Islands participated in the Smithsonian Folk Festival in Washington, DC. Horace was in charge of a crew consisting of 13 chefs representing authentic Virgin Islands cuisine. Horace oversaw all preparation, ordering of food, and organization of the distribution and sanitation of all food during that 21-day period. They averaged serving 3,000 to 4,000 dishes per day.

- **1983 - 1988:** Social Welfare Department, St. Thomas, U.S. Virgin Islands

Position: Kitchen Consultant for St. Thomas, St. Croix, and St. John

- Created seven-cycle menus for all kitchens, providing three meals and two snacks daily.

- Managed food ordering and storage on a quarterly basis.

- Oversaw the food budget for the homes for the aging on all three islands.

- Delivered meals on wheels to homes and recreation centers.

- Participated in vendor selection for food supplies.

- Horace also owned and managed several restaurants and catering services, both in-house and off-premise.

Horace was recognized in the July 2003 issue of *National Culinary Review.*

Horace was diagnosed with muscular dystrophy in 2001 at the age of 45. This diagnosis was a devastating blow, forcing him to rethink what this phase of life would look like. The doctors indicated that it was not a matter of *if,* but *when* he would need to start using a wheelchair to maintain some mobility.

Horace faced the heartbreaking challenge of receiving constant phone calls and visits from friends and customers requesting his services for special occasions. He had also been responsible for preparing food for his church picnic, which served 3,000 people once a year. Ultimately, he had to inform everyone that he could no longer continue doing what he had always taken pride in.

INTRODUCTION

In this book, we aim to introduce some rich, flavorful seasonings featuring unique blends of spices that complement all food groups. Many of these spices are specifically labeled for various types of food, such as chicken seasoning, pork rub, steak seasoning, green seasoning, and more. These labels not only indicate the contents of each jar but also eliminate the guesswork involved in seasoning food, helping you create mouth-watering dishes. Additionally, we include recipes suitable for large parties and family dinners, taking the uncertainty out of preparing meals for gatherings and helping you impress your guests. These larger recipes can also be utilized in restaurant settings.

Horace developed an interest in the culinary arts at an early age. He not only enjoyed different types of food but was also curious about the preparation and blending of flavors. Born in Newport News, Virginia, he moved to St. Thomas, Virgin Islands, as a young boy. There, he began experiencing various foods and unique flavors while being exposed to staple food items from multiple Caribbean cultures. When he was around eight years old, he moved to North Carolina with his grandparents, where he learned about smokehouses, prepared sausages, and enjoyed fresh meats, fruits, and vegetables. He recalls watching chickens run across the yard on Saturdays and then eating the same chicken on Sundays. It was quite an adjustment—this is one of those aspects of life you cannot judge based on today's standards; life was much different in the 1960s.

Horace's first job in the kitchen was preparing sandwiches at a food counter. He soon moved on to work as a dishwasher in a hotel, quickly advancing to a prep cook position and becoming a line cook within two weeks. At that time, cooking was not recognized as a profession; it was considered a trade. It was only through increased travel and more people experiencing diverse culinary cuisines that being a chef began to gain respect as a profession. This field is not suitable for anyone who lacks a passion for food. I encourage anyone interested in the culinary arts to gain experience in the kitchen before making a significant investment in culinary school. Most people only see the finished product in restaurants or on TV; they are often unaware of the heavy lifting, extensive preparation, and the adrenaline rush that chefs experience during service hours.

ABOUT THE BOOK

After much prayer, meditation, and persistent inquiries about food preparation, the idea for "Chef in a Jar" spices emerged. This initiative aims to empower the ordinary cook to become extraordinary.

Get excited! Chef in a Jar offers a selection of spices merged through the experience of many different cuisines—French, Italian, West Indian, Southern, etc. Herbs, spices, and flavorful rubs that enhance all your grilled, broiled, fried, and baked meats, poultry, and seafood dishes.

Our carefully blended herbs and spices provide instant flavor and delicious results, creating a unique flavor profile unlike any other.

Our blended seasonings have been tried and tested in numerous resorts, hotels, and restaurants throughout our chef's 35-year career. After much experimentation, we are now offering the perfect combinations through our Chef in a Jar brand.

We've taken the guesswork out of cooking. The labels clearly indicate which spices to use for beef, pork, seafood, and poultry, making you a star in the kitchen! At Chef in a Jar, we believe that food is about more than just sustenance; it's about bringing people together. That's why we started this small business—to create delicious meals and unforgettable experiences for our customers.

Visit us at chefinajar.net!

PART I
MENUS

REFRESHMENTS

Coffee and Refreshment Service

Assorted Danish, Muffins or Donuts

Assorted Fancy Cookies

Assorted Yogurts

Butter Croissants

Champagne Punch

Chocolate Croissants

Coffee, Brewed Decaf, Tea or Iced Tea

Fruit Kabobs

Fresh Indian River Orange or Grapefruit Juice

Gatorade

Ice Cream Sandwiches

Large Chocolate Chip Cookies

Natural Exotic Tropic Juice (Seasonal)

Perrier with Lime Wedges

Regular & Diet Sodas

Tropical Fruit Punch

Whole or Cut Fresh Fruit Bowl

Break Time

Tropical Day Break

Fresh Cut Fruit Bowl

Assorted Yogurts & Granola Topping

Large Fancy Cookies

Perrier with Lime Wedges

Coffee, Brewed Decaf or Tea

Daily Bread

Fresh Homemade Specialty Bread

(Banana Nut, Date Nut, Orange Loaf..)

Butter, Cream Cheese & Preserves

Fresh Fruit Kabobs

Coffee, Brewed Decaf or Tea

In The Pink

Pink Grapefruit Juice, Orange Juice

and Butter Croissants Fresh Whole Strawberries and

Orange Sections

Coffee, Brewed Decaf or Tea

Bagelmania

Locally made Bagels with your choice

Of the following toppings:

Lox and Cream Cheese and White Wine

Pizza Bagel and Chianti

Reuben Bagel

Florida Continental

Fresh Indian River Orange and

Grapefruit Juice

Assorted Muffins, Danish and

Breakfast Breads

Butter, Preserves & Cream Cheese

Coffee, Brewed Decaf or Tea

Fresh Florida Orange and

Grapefruit Juice

Indian River Orange and

Grapefruit Sections

Fresh or Baked Half Grapefruit

Supreme of Fresh Fruit

Fruit Compote

Sandpiper Continental

Fresh Orange and Grapefruit Juice

Fresh Cut Tropical Fruits

Assorted Fruit Yogurts

Assorted Muffins, Danish Pastries and Breakfast Breads

Butter, Preserves and Cream Cheese

Coffee, Brewed Decaf or Tea

Strawberries, Brown Sugar and

Fresh Cream

Quartered Pineapple

Ripe Melon (Seasonal)

Fruit Yogurt with

Granola Topping

Coffee Breaks & Refreshments

(1a) Freshly Brewed Coffee, Decaffeinated Coffee, Tea, or Milk

(1b) Fresh Orange or Grapefruit Juices

(1c) Soft Drinks

(1d) Half Pints of Milk

(1e) Danish, Pastries, Croissants, Coffee Cakes

(1f) Mineral Waters (Splits)

(1g) Assorted Fancy Cookies

(1h) Assorted Yogurts, Plain or Fruit

(1i) Finger Sandwiches

(1j) Display of Sliced Seasonal Fruit

(2) Country Tea Time

Assorted Imported and Domestic Teas

and Spices served with Butter Cookies

Coffee on Request

(3) The Natural Way

Fresh Dairy Yogurts

Assorted Fresh Fruit with Nut Toppings

Granola Bars served with Coffee,

Decaffeinated Coffee and Tea

(4) Half Time

Hot Dogs with Condiments

Peanuts

(5) The Topper

Top off your meeting reference with a celebration

Mounds of Fresh Fruit to dip in a Chocolate Fondue

(6) Plated Breakfast

(6a) Continental Breakfast

Fresh Orange or Grapefruit

Danish Pastries, Muffins, or Croissants with

Butter, Preserves, & Apple Butter

Coffee, Tea, Freshly Brewed Decaffeinated Coffee, or Milk

(6b) Traditional Scrambled Eggs

Choice of Juice

Link Sausage or Crisp Bacon

Breakfast Potatoes

Danish Pastries, Coffee Cake, or Muffin

With Butter, Preserves, and Apple Butter

Coffee, Tea, Freshly Brewed Decaffeinated Coffee, or Milk

(6c) Traditional Scrambled Eggs

Fruit Cup

Grilled Ham

Breakfast Potatoes

Danish Pastries, or Muffins with Butter,

Preserves, & Apple Butter

Coffee, Tea, Freshly Brewed Decaffeinated

Coffee, or Milk

(6d) Eggs Benedict

Fruit Cup, Poached Eggs on English Muffins,

with Canadian Bacon, & topped with Hollandaise Sauce

Breakfast Potatoes

Danish Pastries or Muffins with Butter,

Preserves, and Apple Butter

Coffee, Tea, Freshly Brewed Decaffeinated Coffee, or Milk

(6e) Fluffy Ham, Cheese or Mushroom Omelet

Buttered Grits or Breakfast Potatoes

Danish Pastries or Coffee Cake with Butter,

Preserves, and Apple Butter

Coffee, Tea, Freshly Brewed

Decaffeinated Coffee, or Milk

(7) Breakfast Buffets

(7a) Breakfast Buffet

Chilled Fruit Juices

Fresh Fruit Juices Compote

Country Style Scrambled Eggs

Crisp Bacon and Link Sausage

Buttered Grits

Breakfast Potatoes

Danish Pastries, Coffee Cake, with Butter, Preserves, and Apple Butter

Coffee, Tea, Freshly Brewed Decaffeinated Coffee, or Milk

(7b) Traditional Scrambled Eggs

Chilled Fruit Juices

Fresh Sliced Fruit with Cheese Wedges

Assortment of Cereals with Seasonal

Berries and Cream

Scrambled Eggs

Corned Beef Hash

Crisp Bacon and Link Sausages

Breakfast Potatoes

Buttered Grits

Danish Pastries, Coffee Cake, or Muffins with Butter, Preserves, and Apple Butter

Coffee, Tea, Freshly Brewed Decaffeinated Coffee, or Milk

The Breakfast Buffet

The Buffet Breakfast

Fresh Orange, Grapefruit and

Tomato Juice

Assorted Cereals

Fresh Orange, Grapefruit

Fluffy Scrambled Eggs

Grilled Link Sausages

Crisp Bacon Branches

Hash Brown Potatoes

Buttered Grits

Sliced Seasonal Fruit & Berries

Assorted Fruit Yogurts

Breakfast Pastries

Butter and Preserves

Beverage

Breakfast Buffet

Fresh Orange, Grapefruit

Tomato and Cranberry Juice

Sliced Seasonal Fruit

Eggs Benedict

Belgium Waffles with

Maple Syrup and Whipped Cream

Quiche du Jour

Corned Beef Hash

Cheese Blintzes with Blueberry Sauce

Crisp Bacon Branches and

Grilled Link Sausages

Bagels with Cream Cheese

Coq au Vin

Fettuccini Neptune

Beef Forestier

Fresh Vegetables du Jour

Assorted Breakfast Pastries and Breads

Butter and Preserves

The Country Breakfast Buffet

Fresh Orange, Grapefruit, Tomato

and Cranberry Juice

Assorted Cereals

Country Scrambled Eggs

Sliced Country Ham

Sausage Patties

Cottage Fried Potatoes

Escalloped Apples

Buttered Grits

Homemade Buttermilk Biscuits

Fresh Fruit & Berries with

Cottage Cheese

Assorted Fruit Yogurts

Breakfast Pastries & Breads

Butter and Preserves

Beverage

As You Like It

Eggs Toppings, Sliced Mushrooms,

Grated Cheddar Cheese, Lox,

Chopped Chives

Eggs Cooked To Your Order

Waffles Cooked To Your Order

Waffles with your favorite toppings

ENTREES

Fluffy Scrambled Eggs with

Crisp Bacon Branches

Grilled Link Sausage &

Hash Brown Potatoes

Swedish Apple Pancakes with

Maple Syrup and

Crisp Bacon Branches

Eggs Benedict

Poached Eggs served on

English Muffin with

Canadian Bacon &

Hollandaise Sauce

Accompanied by Asparagus Tips

and Glazed Peach Half

Grilled French Toast in a

Cornflake Batter served with

Maple Syrup

Accompanied by Canadian Bacon

Country Scrambled Eggs with

Grilled Ham Steak,

Cottage Fried Potatoes and,

Homemade Buttermilk Biscuits

Steak and Eggs

A 6 oz. New York Strip Steak

Served with Scrambled Eggs,

Hash Browns and a

Grilled Tomato

Swiss Cheese, & Salami – Hard Roll

Hard Boiled Egg

Banana Cake

Apple

Jumbo Gulf Shrimp

Tuna Salad- Whole Wheat Bread

Hard Boiled Eggs

Creamy Cole Slaw

Sun-Ripened Orange

Carrot Cake

Imported Ham & Cheddar Cheese – Rye Bread

Broiled Chicken Breast

Hard Boiled Eggs

Banana Cake

Apple

Luncheon No. 1

Caribbean Seafood Bisque

Fresh Fruit Salad Plate

(Assorted Fresh Fruit with

Cottage Cheese, Yogurt, or Sherbet)

Rum Mousse

Luncheon No. 2

Gazpacho Andalouse

Breast of Capon Oscar

Rice Pilaf

Chilled Mousse

Luncheon No. 3

Chilled Melon & Prosciutto Ham

Island Pepper Steak

Rice Pilaf

Vegetables Polonaise

Black Forest Cake

Luncheon No. 4

French Onion Soup

Fresh Avocado Half, filled

with Shrimp Salad

Strawberry Cheesecake

Luncheon No. 5

Egg Drop Soup

Chilled Poached Salmon

Oriental Rice & Vegetables

Almond Float with

Mandarin Oranges

Luncheon No. 6

Rich Cream of Mushroom Soup

Reef Cold Plate

(Roast Beef, Soppressata,

Breast of Turkey, Pate,

Cheddar Cheese) Deviled Eggs,

Nicoise Vegetable Salad

Apple Cake

Luncheon No. 7

Lobster Bisque

Fisherman's Plate

(Avocado with Crabmeat, Smoked Dolphin,

Jumbo Shrimp garnished with Asparagus,

Hearts of Palm & Artichokes)

Coffee, Iced Tea.

Light Luncheons

Assorted Seasonal Fruit Platter with Honey

Yogurt Dressing

Deli Platter

Prime Rib Sandwich on Dark Rye

Broiled Crab Cake Sandwich

Luncheons

Quiche Lorraine

Breast of Chicken Hunter Style

Brisket of Beef with Horseradish Sauce

Beef Stroganoff

Seafood Newburg on Rice Pilaf

Braised Filet of Flounder Meuniere

Veal Parmigiana

Luncheon Buffets

Buffet of Southern Style Fried Chicken,

Beef Stroganoff, & Buttered Noodles

Buffet of Shrimp Creole, Chicken Tenders

Scampi, Barbecued Short Ribs, Rice Pilaf,

Squash, Zucchini & Red Bell Peppers

Buffet of Top Round of Beef, Medallions of

Veal Marsala, Potatoes Parisienne,

Fresh Seasonal Vegetables

The Cookout

From the Grill:

Fresh Ground Hamburgers

Jumbo Kosher Hot Dogs

Sautéed Onions & Mushrooms

Chili con Carne

American & Swiss Cheeses

Sauerkraut & Bacon Bits

Lettuce & Sliced Tomatoes

Kosher Dill Pickles

Potato Salad

Mexican Corn Salad

Chocolate Brownies

Sliced Watermelon

Coffee or Iced Tea

Hero Sandwich Buffet

From the carving board,

We will cut the desired length

Of a three-foot

Italian Hero Sandwich

Artichoke Salad with Feta Cheese

Pasta Salad Primavera

Carrot Salad

Fresh Sliced Fruit

Napoleons

Coffee or Iced Tea

The Deli

Soup du Jour

Platter of lean Corned Beef, Baked Ham,

Breast of Turkey, Roast Beef,

American and Swiss Cheeses

Assorted Deli Breads and Rolls

Lettuce, Sliced Tomatoes and

Kosher Dill Pickles

Waldorf Salad

German Potato Salad

Cole Slaw

Carrot Cake

Coffee or Iced Tea

The Chicken and Rib Buffet

Tossed Garden Salad

Choice of dressing

Texas Style Sliced Tomatoes

Relish Tray

Honey Dipped Fried Chicken

Barbecued Back Ribs

Corn on the Cob

Baked Beans with Bacon

Skilled Corn Bread

Sliced Watermelon

Pecan Pie

Beverage

Boxed Lunches

Roast Beef Sandwich on Croissant

Cheese Wedge & Crackers

Hard Boiled Egg

Potato Chips

Whole Fresh Fruit

One Cookie

One Half Each

Roast Beef, Ham and Cheese

And Turkey Breast Sandwich

Potato Chips

Chocolate Brownie

Whole Fresh Fruit

Cold Fried Chicken

Celery and Carrot Sticks

Cheese and Crackers

Hard Boiled Egg

Cole Slaw

Fresh Fruit

Two Cookies

Luncheon No. 1

Appetizer

Fresh Fruit Compote with Madori, Assorted Relishes

Cold Dishes

Genoa Salami, Soppressata Sausage,

Sliced Breast of Turkey, Baked Sugar Cured Ham,

Tortellini Primavera, Chicken Liver Paté, Deviled Eggs

Hot Chafing Dishes

Fresh Fish West Indian Style

London Broil – Mushroom Sauce

Deep Fried Chicken

Salads

Lettuce Salad, Vegetable Salad

Desserts

Pastries & Cakes, Freshly Brewed Coffee,

Decaffeinated Coffee, Herbal Tea, Milk

Luncheon No. 2

Appetizers

Fresh Fruit Compote with Madori, Chilled Melon Slices,

Assorted Relishes

Cold Dishes

Sliced Roast Turkey, Sliced Breast of Turkey,

Baked Sugar Cured Ham, Conch Ceviche, Poached Salmon

Chicken Liver Paté, Deviled Eggs

Hot Chafing Dishes

London Broil – Mushroom Sauce

Red Snapper – Lemon Butter

Sautéed Chicken Cutlets

Salads

Mixed Green Salad, Nicoise Vegetable Salad, Barcelona Salad

Desserts

Pastries & Cakes, Freshly Brewed Coffee

Decaffeinated Coffee, Herbal Tea, Milk

Pub Lunch Buffet

Cold

Assorted Relish Tray, Deviled Eggs, Potato Salad,

Cole Slaw, Pineapple & Coconut Compote, Tomato & Onion Vinaigrette, Sliced Paté, Meats & Cheese

(Roast Beef, Boiled Ham, Turkey Breast, Liver Paté, Cheddar Cheese)

Dessert

Lemon Mousse

Freshly Brewed Coffee, Decaffeinated Coffee,

Herbal Tea, Milk

Suggested Beverage

Punch or Ice Tea

Fierá Lunch Buffet

Antipasto

Fresh Romaine, Mushrooms, Cherry Peppers, Carrots,
Olives, Anchovies, Celery, Tomatoes, Hardboiled Eggs,
Melon, Peperonchini, Capers, Spring Onions, Radishes,
Cucumbers, Olive Oil, Wine Vinegar, Parmesan Cheese

Cold

Genoa Salami, Soppressata Sausage, Pepperoni, Prosciutto, Provolone Cheese, Tuna Vinaigrette

Hot

Sweet Fennel Sausage, Garlic Bread

Desserts

Lemon Mousse

Freshly Brewed Coffee, Decaffeinated Coffee

Herbal Tea, Milk

<u>Hot Buffets</u>

1. Baked herbal Chicken

   Seasonal Rice

   Mixed Vegetables

   Rolls & Butter

   Assorted Cakes

2. Buffalo Wings

   BBQ Meatballs

   Vegetable Tray w/Dip

   Breads

   Assorted Cookies

<u>Cold Buffet</u>

3. Toss Green Salad

   Tomatoes/Cucumbers

   Chicken Salad

   Pasta Salad

   Cookies

4. Cheese w/crackers

   Tuna Macaroni Salad

   Salted Dry Snacks

   Nuts & Mints

   Strawberry Short Cake

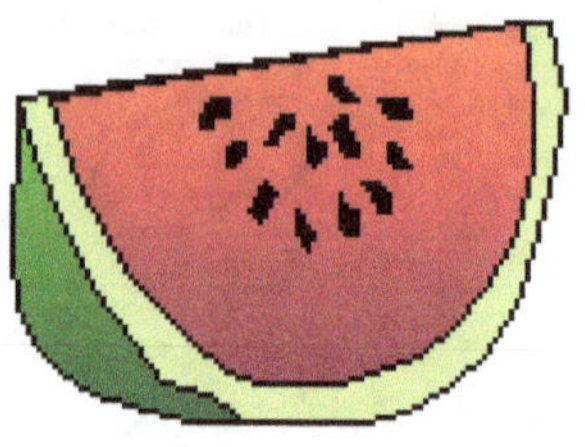

The Working Lunch

Some Sandwiches (suggestions)

Finely minced egg, tuna, chicken, or shrimp salad, on buttered white or whole wheat breads,

Thin slices of ripe tomato, spread with a bit of avocado cream, on whole wheat bread, cut.

Wheat bread, spread with cream cheese, topped with wafers of slated and drained cucumber.

Herb butter, spread on thin bread, rolled around a sprig of watercress, cheese and tomatoes.

Assorted Rolls

Turkey, Ham, Chicken, Salami, Beef, Cheese, Fetti cheese, beef pastrami

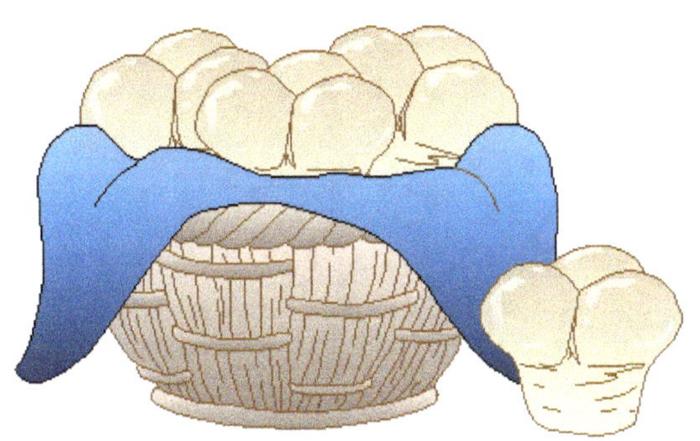

Chafing Dishes

Hors d'oeuvres

Sausage Roll

Deep Fried Chicken Legs

Quiche Lorraine

Shrimp Fritter

Pumpkin Quiche

Pineapple in Boston

Miniature Pizzas

Chicken Livers in Bacon

Crab Quiche

Barbecued Meatballs

Snails in Garlic Butter

Deep Fried Chicken Wings

Italian Sausage

Stuffed Mushrooms

Crisp Fried Mushrooms

Egg Rolls

Scallops in Bacon

Crisp Fried Zucchini

Fried Scallops

Swedish Meatballs

Oriental Chicken Wings

Assorted Puff Pastry

Conch Fritter

Fried Cheese

Crab Balls

Fried Oysters

Tortellini Crisps

Deep Fried Jumbo Shrimp

Beef Wellington

Escargot in Puff Pastry

Fried Wonton

Cold Dishes

Hors d'oeuvres

Eggs a la Russe

Danish Ham

Smoked Oysters

Deviled Crab

Sliced Egg Caviar

Deviled Shrimp

Ham Rolls with Horseradish

Celery Hearts and Blue Cheese

Jumbo Shrimp

Stuffed Cherry Tomatoes

Crab Fingers

Deviled Curried Chicken

Salami Comucopias

Cream Cheese and Walnut

Smoked Salmon

Mushrooms a la Greque

Scallops Ceviche

Artichoke Hearts Vinaigrette

Soppressata

Sushi

Lobster Pinwheels

Chicken and Almond Ribbons

Club Cheese Pinwheels

RECEPTIONS

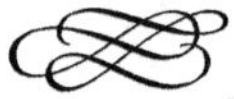

The Governor's Reception

Smoked Salmon Station

Slices of Smoked Salmon sliced by Chef with Onions,

Capers, Chopped Eggs served with Bagel Thins

Canapés

A gourmet selection of Canapés presented on silver trays

served butler style

Chafing Dish Selection

Escargot in Puffed Pastry, Baked Stuffed Mushrooms,

Clams Casino, Filet of Beef Wellington

Flambé

Jumbo Shrimp flambéed with Cognac & Spices

The President's Reception

Raw Bar

Clams on the Half Shell, Jumbo Gulf Shrimp,

Lobster Medallions, Poached Curried Mussels

Tenderloin of Beef Station

Prime Tenderloin of Beef Roasted Rare & served sliced to

order with Béarnaise Sauce & French Bread

Cheese Board

Variety of International Cheeses served with Carr's Water

Table Biscuits

Hors d'oeuvres

Fancy Cold Canapés

Jumbo Shrimp on Sliced Egg, Smoked Scottish Salmon, Lobster Mousse,

Deviled Crab, Imported Caviar

The Raw Bar

Clams on the Half Shell, Oysters on the Half Shell

Lobster Display

Slices of Caribbean Lobster presented on Mirror with Whole Lobster Centerpiece

International Cheese Board

Variety of Domestic & Imported Cheeses served with

Stoneground Wafers & Carr's Water Table Biscuits

Crudités

Seasonal Selection of Fresh Cut Vegetables served with Dill Sauce

Shrimp Flambé

Jumbo Shrimp flambéed with Cognac & Spices

Tenderloin of Beef

Prime Tenderloin of Beef Roasted Rare & sliced to order with

Béarnaise Sauce & French Bread

Hot Seafood

Clams Casino, Oysters Rockefeller, Dartois or Crabmeat in Puffed Pastry

(both sliced to order)

Finger Treats

A variety of Dry Salted Snacks

Featuring: Mixed Nuts, Corn Chips, Pretzels, Potato Chips

Special Dips with Chips

A variety of freshly prepared Vegetable Dips with Tortilla Chips

Featuring: Chili con Queso, Guacamole, French Onion

Gourmet Combinations

Combinations of Imported Variety Meats & Cheeses

Featuring: Pepperoni & Provolone, Salami & Provolone,

Cream Cheese & Prosciutto

Stand Up Buffet

Continental Table

(Crudités, Sausages, Marinated Vegetables)

Mushrooms a la Greque, Marinated Eggs, pepperoni, Genoa Salami, Cherry Peppers,

Prosciutto, Seasonal Melon & Fruit, Ripe & Green Olives, Julienne of Chicken Breast,

Soppressata, Tuna Fish Vinaigrette, Bread Sticks, & Garlic Toast

European Table

Smoked Scotch Salmon sliced to order, Capers, Chopped Onions, Parsley,

Chopped Egg Whites & Yolks, Diced Tomatoes, Cream Cheese, Toasted Bagel Thins

Cheese Board

(Bruder Basil, Routhier with Pistachio, Borichampi, Provolone, Stone Ground Wafers, Seasonal Grapes)

The Bar

A consumption bar

Carving Station

Rare Prime Tenderloin

Smoked Bone-in Ham

Sliced to order on French & Whole Wheat Rolls

Béarnaise, Horseradish, & Spicy Mustard Sauce

Hot Selections

Petite Quiche Lorraine

French Fried Zucchini, Dill Sauce

Shrimp, Scallops, & Artichokes Sauté

Braised Peppers, Onions & Sausage Salpicon

Desert Station

Assorted Strudels, French Pastries, Cakes & Cookies

Flaming Coffee Station

Irish, Jamaican, Italian, Grand Marnier

54

SPECIAL

Hors d'oeuvres

Assorted Cold Canapés (priced per 100 pieces)

Stuffed Celery with Roquefort Prosciutto Ham with Melon Assorted Finger Sandwiches Crabmeat in Mushroom Caps

Deviled Eggs

Smoked Salmon

Domestic Caviar Canapés

Hot Hors d'oeuvres

(priced per 100 pieces)

Miniature Quiche Lorraine

Chinese Egg roll with Hot Mustard Sauce

Cocktail Franks in Pastry Blankets

Fried Chicken Tenders Fried Breaded Shrimp

Fried Oysters with Sauce Piquant Beef, Seafood or Chicken Kebobs

Cheese Puffs

Teriyaki Brochettes

Barbecued Spare Ribs

Specialty Items

(priced per 100 pieces)

Barbecued Gulf Shrimp

Tenderloin Tips in Perigourdine
Sauce

Crab Claws

Specialty Receptions

Steamship Round of Beef au jus

Baked Glazed Ham

Smoked Salmon

Tenderloin of Beef Whole Roasted Turkey

Whole Roasted Prime Rib of Beef

International Cheese Display

Vegetable Crudité - Raw

The Seafood Bar

Oysters and Clams

Stone Crab Claws or Iced

Jumbo Shrimp

Dry Snacks

Potato Chips and Pretzels

Deluxe Mixed Nuts

Peanuts

Assortment of Dry Snacks

DINNER MENUS

Roast Prime Rib of Beef

Shrimp Cocktail

Caesar Salad

Roast Prime Rib of Beef (Au Jus)

Baked Potato (Sour Cream)

Fresh Broccoli

Strawberry Cheesecake

Coffee

Chicken Engenie

Fresh Pineapple & `Mandarin Oranges

(Toasted Coconut & Almonds)

Mixed Garden Greens (Thousand Island Dressing)

Sautéed Chicken Breast, Prosciutto Ham, Mushroom Cap

(Light Cream & Sherry Sauce)

Rice Pilaf, Broiled Tomato, Stuffed Zucchini

Chocolate Mousse

Coffee

Sautéed Shrimp

Artichoke Hearts Gratinee

(Hollandaise Sauce, Parmesan Cheese)

hearts of Romaine

(Walnut Vinaigrette)

Sautéed Shrimp

(Butter, Onions, Paprika, White Whine)

Rice Pilaf, Julienne of Fresh Vegetables, Snow Peas

Chocolate Profiterole

(Cream Puffs, Chocolate Sauce)

Coffee

Dinner Menus

Roast Top Sirloin of Beef

Melon & Prosciutto Ham

Hearts of Lettuce

(French Dressing With Herbs)

Roast Top Sirloin of Beef

(Mushroom Sauce)

Oven Roasted Potatoes, Broccoli, Cherry Tomatoes

Roman Apple Cake, Walnuts, Fresh Whipped Cream

Coffee

Caribbean Fresh Fish

Marinated Conch in Lime Juice

(Shrimp Garnish)

Mixed Garden Greens (Thousand Island Dressing)

Caribbean Fresh Fish Fillet, Native Style

(Tomato, Onion, Pepper, & White Whine)

Roasted Carrots, Steamed Plantains

Okra Fungi

(Cornmeal & Okra)

Pitch Lake Pudding

(Mocha Mousse with Orange Liqueur)

Coffee

Roast Rack of Lamb

Scallops Remoulade

Caesar Salad

Roast Rack of Lamb

(Mustard, Fine Herbs, Au Jus)

Selection of Fresh Vegetables

(Broccoli, Tomato, Carrots, Cauliflower)

Small Roasted Potatoes

Chocolate Cheesecake

Coffee

Gala Dinner

Menu No. 1

MELON ET JAMBON DE PARME

Melon & Prosciutto Ham

LAITUE DE BOSTON A LA VINAIGRETTE

Boston Bibb Lettuce with Walnut Vinaigrette

CANARD A L´ORANGE

Crisp Roasted Duckling with Zesty Orange Sauce

or

SOLE MEUNIERE A L'ORANGE

Dover Sole Sautéed in Butter with Oranges

ZIZANIE

Wild Rice

CHOUX ROUGE AUX POMMES BRAISE

Braised Red Cabbage with Apples

CREPES SIMON

Cherry Flavored Crepes with Frangipane Cream

CAFÉ

Coffee

Gala Dinner

Menu No. 2

CROUTE D'ESCARGOT SOUBISE

Imported Snails, Onions, White Wine Sauce

SALADE DE CHAMPIGNONS ET COEURS DE PALMIER

Hearts of Palm & Mushroom Salad

CHATEUBRIAND COLBERT

Tenderloin of Beef, Demi-glace, Lemon, Madeira

or

QUEUE DE LANGOUSTE GRILLE, FILET DE BOEUF

Broiled Lobster Tail, Tenderloin of Beef

BOUQUETIERE DE LEGUMES

Selection of Fresh Vegetables

FRAISES ROMANOFF

Strawberries with Vanilla Ice Cream & Grand Marnier

CAFÉ

Coffee

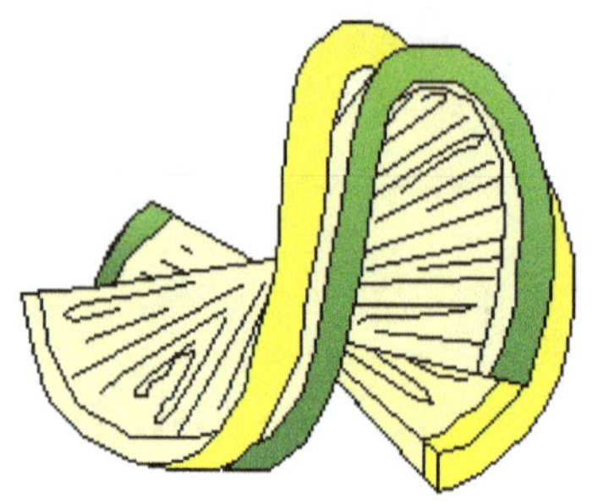

HARBOUR CRUISE PARTY

Harbour Dinner Buffet

Garden Market Table

Smoked Oysters, Green Ripe Olives, Cherry Peppers,

Hearts of Palm, Celery & Carrot Sticks, Radishes,

Scallions, Zucchini, Broccoli, Pepperoni, Salami, Provolone,

Prosciutto, Tuna, Anchovies, Potatoes Vinaigrette,

Deviled Eggs, Blue Cheese, Marinated Mushrooms & Artichokes, Pickled Eggplant, Tortellini Primavera, Tomato,

Melon, Lemon, Seasonings, Oil & Vinegar, Romaine & Iceberg Lettuce

Captain's Catch

Steamed Shrimp & Scallops, Marinated & Chilled,

served with Three Sauces

Steamship Round of Beef Carved to order & served

with Clam Size Rolls, Horseradish, Béarnaise Sauce, &

Sliced Onions

Chocolate Nut Brownies & Coconut Tarts

Special - Dinner

Dinners

Boneless Breast of Chicken Cordon Bleue

Filet of Flounder Meuniere

New York Sirloin Steak

Maryland Crab Cakes

Filet of Beef Wellington

Dinner Buffets

Buffet with Seafood Newburg, Chicken Sautéed with Herbs, Baked Glazed Ham, & Steamship Round of Beef Au Jus

Buffet with Marinated Seafood Salad, Decorated Sliced Ham, Seafood Cardinal, Casino, Medallions of Veal Marsala, Roast Prime Rib of Beef

Italian Dinner Buffet

Meas D'Antipasti

Insalata Mista di Lettuga e Romaine

Pomodori e Cipolle in Salsa Marinata

Funghi in Salamoia

Peperonchini

Pecorino Romano

Formaggio Provolone

Salami de Genoa

Melanzane in Salamoia

Olive Mature e Verde

Certrioli Fetti

Alici A Scapece

Piccata di Vitello al Limone

Costolette Griglia Di Tenderloin

Rigatoni alla Formaggio e Sassie

Verdura Lasagne

Pollo alla Polognese

Melanzane Fritte

Funghi e Fagiolini all'Aglio Olio

Pasticerra

Clacioni All' Ascolana

Cannoli

Torta Shrisulona All' Marasca

Antipasto Table

Tossed Lettuce & Romaine Salad

Tomato Wedges & Onion in Marinade

Pickled Mushrooms

Hot Peppers

Romano Cheese

Provolone Cheese

Genoa Salami

Pickled Eggplant

Ripe Green Olives

Sliced Cucumber

Marinated Anchovies

Veal Piccata with Lemon

Grilled Pork Tenderloin

Rigatoni with Cheese & Sausage

Vegetable Lasagne

Chicken with Meat Sauce

Fried Eggplant

Mushrooms, Green Beans, Garlic & Olive Oil

75

Desserts

Little Cheesecakes

A pastry filled with vanilla & chocolate cream

A layered almond cake with cherries

PART II
RECIPES

BREAD RECIPES

BREAD

Ingredients:

- 5 lb bread flour
- 5 qt milk
- 5 ½ oz yeast

Directions:

Step 1: Mix all together. Milk must be 90 degrees F. Let rise until center is slightly collapsed (approximately 1 hour)

- 15 lb all purpose flour
- 2 oz salt
- 1 cup warm water
- ¾ qt butter

Step 2: Dissolve salt in water then add other ingredients and work with dough hook until ball is formed and does not stick to side of bowl.

Let rise 1½ times or until fill up 60 quart bowl. Work again with dough hook for 5 minutes. Let rise for 15 minutes then form desired shape and brush with egg wash (egg and water). Let rise 1 ½ then bake at 350 degrees F for approximately 20 minutes. When out of oven, spray with butter.

Note: For rye bread instead of bread flour add rye flour and it may need to rise a little more.

CORN MUFFINS

<u>Ingredients:</u>

- 14 lb milk
- 5 lb oil
- 6 lb eggs
- 8 lb cornmeal
- 15 lb all-purpose flour
- 1 lb 4 oz baking powder
- 6 oz salt
- 10 lb sugar
- 4 tbsp black pepper

FRIED JOHNNY CAKES

Ingredients:

- 5 lb flour
- 3 tbsp baking powder
- 1 tbsp salt
- 1 cup sugar
- ½ lb crisco
- 1 can milk
- 32 oz water

Preparations:

1. Sift flour, baking powder, and salt
2. Cut in shortening
3. Add water and canned milk
4. Knead until smooth
5. Roll 1/4 inch thick
6. Cut in rounds and prick with fork
7. Fry in hot deep fat
8. Serve hot

HUSH PUPPYS

Ingredients:

- 2 lb yellow corn meal
- 1 lb white flour
- 6 eggs
- 24 oz buttermilk
- 2 ½ tsp Lowreys seasoned salt.
- 1 tbsp ground pepper
- 1 tsp baking powder
- 1 oz baking soda
- 3 oz bacon grease.
- 2 oz white sugar

Preparations:

1. Mix all of the dry ingredients in a bowl
2. Add your eggs, oil, and buttermilk
3. Stir it all up until the flavors are thoroughly blended
4. Before cooking, let it reach near room temperature

LOCAL ISLAND DUMB BREAD

Dumb refers to a style of cooking used in India to make bread. Virgin Islanders would place coals in the bottom of a coal pot. Then, bread dough was put in a cast iron skillet and placed on top of the coals. Then over the pot, there was a metal sheet with more coals on top. Over the years, the named changed to dumb.

Yield: 60 servings

Nutrition: 272 calories, 11 grams fat, 2 milligrams cholesterol and 388 milligrams sodium *per one-tenth loaf serving (with coconut).*

<u>Ingredients:</u>

- 5 lb all-purpose flour
- 1 qt water
- 12 oz sugar
- 4 oz Crisco
- 1 can evaporated milk
- 1 lb margarine or butter
- 1 lb shortening
- 6 oz baking powder
- 1 lb dried shredded coconut, if desired

<u>Method:</u>

In a large mixing bowl, combine all ingredients to form dough. On a floured surface, knead the dough until smooth, or about 10 to 15 minutes. (Dough will be somewhat stiff.) Divide dough into six pieces. Roll each piece into a ball, and then flatten slightly with the palm of the hand. Place loaves on a greased baking sheet. Bake in a pre-heated 350° oven for 35 to 40 minutes or until browned. When done, cut into ten wedges.

PLACE PIZZA DOUGH RECIPE

<u>Ingredients:</u>

- 28 lb Water
- 14 oz Salt
- 14 oz Dry yeast
- 4 oz Malt syrup
- 16 oz Olive oil
- 32 oz High Gluden flour
- 10 oz Semolina flour

APPETIZERS

ANNATO-GARLIC BUTTER

Ingredients:

- Whole Butter (5 lb) – cut into cubes and allow butter to get room temperature
- Medium Garlic Cloves (4 oz)
- Annato Seed (4 tbsp)
- Salt (1/4 cup)
- Aged Sherry Vinegar (1 cup)
- Virgin Olive Oil (4 oz)

Directions:

1. Heat garlic, oil, and annatto seed in a small saucepan over low heat until the garlic is roasted and golden brown.
2. Add vinegar and salt, and purée in blender until smooth.
3. Combine all ingredients and whip in mixer.
4. Divide into five parts.
5. Use wax paper to roll into cylinders and wrap each cylinder in plastic.
6. Freeze.

BASIL GARLIC BUTTER

Ingredients:

- 5 lb   butter (soft)
- 1 tbsp   w pepper
- 1 tbsp   salt
- 2 oz   lemon juice
- 4 oz   anisette
- 4 oz   garlic
- 10 oz   basil (fresh leaves only)

Directions:

In a mixing bowl, using paddle, mix butter; salt; lemon juice and anisette until whipped well.

CEASAR DRESSING

Ingredients:

- Egg Yolks (32 each)
- 10 lbs 8 oz Olive Oil
- 10 lbs 8 oz Salad Oil
- 8 oz Garlic minced

- 3 lbs Lemon Juice
- 8 oz Red Wine Vinegar
- 2.2 oz Black Pepper
- 2 lbs Anchovy
- 2 lbs Water
- 2 lbs Parmesan grated

Preparations:

1. Pour slowly while whisking
2. Place first seven ingredients in robot and whirl until smooth
3. Transfer to mixing bowl
4. Add cheese and mix thoroughly

COLESLAW MIX

Ingredients:

- Green Cabbage
- Carrots

Instructions:

1. Slice the cabbage and shred the carrots.

2. Combine the shredded cabbage and carrots in a mixing bowl and mix well.

3. Prepare the dressing with the following ingredients:

- Mayonnaise: 1 gallon
- Cider vinegar: 1 cup
- Sugar: ½ lb
- Celery seed: 2 oz
- Salt: 1 tbsp
- White pepper: 1 tbsp

4. Pour the dressing over the cabbage and carrot mixture, then mix well to combine all the ingredients.

Enjoy your coleslaw!

MARYLAND CRABCAKES
AWARD-WINNING RECIPE

yields: 15 crabcakes

Ingredients:

- 2 lb jumbo lump crabmeat
- 1 lb flounder fillet, cooked and chopped
- 4 slices of white bread, chopped

- 3 large eggs, beaten
- 3 tbsp Old Bay Seasoning
- 1 tsp garlic powder
- Juice of 1 lemon (seeds removed)
- 1/2 cup mayonnaise
- 1 tbsp Dijon-style prepared mustard
- 1 tbsp Worcestershire sauce
- 1/4 cup chopped parsley
- 1 tsp chopped chervil
- 1 tsp black pepper

Directions:

1. Place the crabmeat in a large bowl and remove any remaining shell pieces.
2. Break the bread into small pieces and add it to the bowl with the crabmeat and flounder.
3. Add the beaten eggs, New Bay seasoning, mayonnaise, mustard, Worcestershire sauce and all remaining ingredients to the bowl. Mix gently by hand to avoid overworking the crabmeat; you want to keep the lumps of meat intact. Form the mixture into 15 patties.
4. Heat butter in a skillet over medium heat.
5. Fry the patties in the hot butter until they are golden brown, about 4 minutes per side. Alternatively, you can roll the crabcakes into

balls, pour melted butter over each, and bake in a 350°F oven until golden brown.

Enjoy your delicious crabcakes!

OKRA FUNGI

Ingredients:

- 10 oz package frozen cut okra
- 2½ cups boiling water
- 1½ cups fine yellow cornmeal
- 2 tbsp butter
- ¼ tsp salt pepper, to taste

FUNGI

Ingredients:

- 1 gallon boiling water
- 1 tsp salt
- 1 tsp pepper
- 2 lb corn meal
- 8 oz butter

<u>Directions:</u>

1. To rapidly boiling water add salt.
2. Soak cornmeal in cold water for about 10 minutes and sprinkle cornmeal in slowly.
3. Allow water to boil over meal for a few minutes.
4. Stir briskly to prevent lumping.
5. When well combined, add butter.
6. Cover and steam for about 5 minutes, stirring occasionally.

SOUPS

CONCH CHOWDER

Yield: 4 Gallon

Ingredients:

- 4 qt fish stock or clam juice
- 4 lb potatoes, diced
- 4 whole yellow onions, chopped
- 1.5 lb celery, chopped
- 3 large carrots, chopped
- ½ cup garlic, minced
- 3 lb conch, chopped
- ½ lb butter
- 1 can (No. 10) diced tomatoes
- 1.5 tbsp Old Bay seafood seasoning
- 1.5 tbsp thyme
- 1 tbsp oregano
- juice from 3 fresh limes
- 1 tbsp cayenne pepper
- 1.5 tbsp white pepper
- 1.5 tbsp black pepper
- 1.5 tbsp parsley, chopped
- salt to taste

Directions:

1. Cook Potatoes in Fish Stock until potatoes are barely done.
2. Sauté Vegetables and Conch in Butter.
3. Combine Potatoes & Stock, sautéed Vegetables & Conch with remaining ingredients.
4. Bring to a boil, and simmer for 30 minutes.
5. Adjust seasonings, if needed.

Serving Ideas: Serve with a TB of sherry in each bowl

OXTAIL RECIPE

Ingredients:

- 4 lb oxtails
- 2 large onions, chopped
- 3 scallions, chopped
- 4 garlic cloves, minced
- 1 bunch fresh thyme
- 1 Scotch bonnet pepper/or habanero
- 1 tsp Ground all spice
- 2 tsp Ground cloves
- 4 tsp paprika

- 1 bay leaves
- 1 tbsp Nora Swiss beef base
- 2 tbsp tomato paste
- 2 tbsp salt

<u>Directions:</u>

1. In a large pot, add oxtails, onions, scallions, garlic, thyme, red pepper, paprika, bay leaf, hot pepper, and all dry spices and marinate at least 4 hours or overnight in the refrigerator, stirring occasionally.

2. Add enough water to just cover the oxtails and bring the mixture to a boil. Lower to a simmer, cover and cook 2 hours. Every 30 minutes for 2 hours add 2 cups of water keep oxtails covered with liquid.

3. At 2 hours, tomato paste, and 2 more cups of water, if needed. Bring to a boil then simmer uncovered 2 hours, skimming fat off top and stirring occasionally. In the last 1/2 hour of cook time, season with 2 tablespoons salt. Serve with rice.

MAIN DISHES

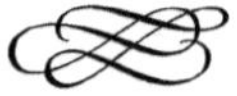

ANNATO-GARLIC STEAK MARINADE

Yield: 4 logs

Ingredients:

- 1 white onion
- 20 pc medium garlic cloves
- 4 tsp annatto seed
- ¼ cup salt
- 1 cup aged sherry vinegar
- 4 oz blended oil

Preparation:

1. Steep garlic, oil, and annatto seed in a small saucepan over low heat until the garlic is roasted.
2. Add onions, cook for 2 minutes.
3. Add vinegar and salt, and purée in blender until smooth.

ASIAGO CHEESE AND GARLIC POTATOES

Ingredients:

- 4 large baking potatoes, about 2 pounds, peeled and cut into 1-inch pieces or instant potato flakes
- 1 cup heated heavy cream or milk
- 2 tbsp butter, room temperature
- 4 oz asiago cheese
- 1/4 tsp ground black pepper
- 1/4 tsp salt
- 1/4 tsp garlic

Preparation:

1. Cook potatoes in boiling water until tender, about 15 minutes.
2. Drain well.
3. Put potatoes back in saucepan; stir over low heat until dry, about 2 minutes.
4. Remove from heat.
5. Mash, adding about 1/2 cup milk and the 2 tablespoons butter.
6. Add grated cheese and seasonings.
7. Beat with a spoon, adding remaining milk until desired consistency is reached.

8. Serves 4.

BAKED MAC AND CHEESE

Ingredients:

- elbow macaroni

- butter

- flour

- 1 half cube chicken base

- 1 pint heavy cream

- ½ pint water

- 1 bay leaf

- 8 oz sharp cheddar, shredded

- sea salt

- black pepper

- ½ bunch chopped parsley

Topping: 2 tbsp butter

<u>Directions:</u>

1. Preheat oven to 350 degrees F.

2. In a large pot of boiling, salted water cook the pasta to al dente.

3. While the pasta is cooking, in a separate pot, melt the butter. Whisk in the flour and keep it moving for about five minutes. Make sure it's free of lumps. Stir in the milk, water, bay leaf. Simmer for ten minutes and remove the bay leaf.

4. Stir in 3/4 of the cheese. Season with salt and pepper.

5. Fold the macaroni into the mix and pour into a 2-quart casserole dish. Top with remaining cheese.

6. Melt the butter in a sauté pan and toss the bread crumbs to coat. Top the macaroni with the bread crumbs and parsley.

7. Bake for 30 minutes. Remove from oven and rest for five minutes before serving.

BEEF WELLINGTON

Ingredients:

- 2 1/2 lb beef tenderloin
- 2 tbsp butter, softened or olive oil
- 2 tbsp butter
- 1 onion, chopped
- 1/2 cup sliced fresh mushrooms
- 2 oz liver pâté
- 2 tbsp butter, softened
- salt and pepper to taste
- 1 (17.5 oz) package frozen puff pastry, thawed
- 1 egg yolk, beaten
- 10 oz beef broth
- ½ cup red wine

Check All Add to Shopping List

Prep time: 30 minutes, cook for 30 minutes, and ready in 1 hour.

Directions:

1. Preheat oven to 425 degrees F (220 degrees C).
2. Place beef in a hot skillet, and spread with 2 tablespoons softened butter. Cook for 10 to 15 minutes, or until browned on each side.

3. Remove from pan, and allow to cool completely. Save pan juices.
4. Melt 2 tablespoons butter in a skillet over medium heat.
5. Sauté onion and mushrooms in butter for 5 minutes. Remove from heat, and let cool.
6. Mix together pâté and 2 tablespoons softened butter, and season with salt and pepper.
7. Spread pâté over beef. Top with onion and mushroom mixture.
8. Roll out the puff pastry dough, and place beef in the center.
9. Fold up, and seal all the edges.
10. Place beef in a 9x13 inch baking dish, cut a few slits in the top of the dough, and brush with egg yolk.
11. Bake at 425 degrees F (220 degrees C) for 20 to 25 minutes, or until pastry is golden brown.
12. Set aside, and keep warm.
13. Place all reserved juices in a small saucepan over high heat.
14. Stir in beef stock and red wine; boil for 10 to 15 minutes, or until slightly reduced.
15. Strain, and serve with beef.

BUTTERFISH SUNDAY BRUNCH

- Green Salad
- Bacon Strips
- Sausage Links
- Home Fried Potatoes
- Scrambled Eggs
- Banana Pancakes
- Cheese Grits
- Caribbean & Rice
- Fried Chicken
- Fried Fish Creole
- Crab and Rice
- Fresh Fruit
- Cakes

LASAGNA MEAT

4 to 5 1/2 Size, 2 1/2" Deep pans

Step (1)

- 10 lb Ground Beef

Step (2)

- 1 Stalk Celery simmer for 5 minutes
- 2 large Carrots
- 3 large Onions: all diced
- 1.5 oz black pepper, 2 oz salt, 3 bay leaf

Step (3)

- 2 oz Oregano simmer for 2 minutes
- 2 oz Basil
- 2 oz Thyme all chopped

Step (4)

- 7 lb Mozzarella Cheese
- 5 lb Parmesan Cheese
- 7 lb Ricotta Cheese
- 1.5 qt Heavy Whipping Cream
- 1 oz salt
- 1 oz black pepper
- 2 oz Oregano
- ½ oz dried parsley

Directions:

1. In a large skillet over medium heat brown the

ground beef. Add 4gal marinara sauce and simmer for 5 minutes.

2. In a large bowl, mix together spices cream, ricotta cheese, mozzarella cheese, half of the grated Parmesan cheese, dried parsley, salt, oregano and ground black pepper.

3. To assemble, in the bottom of a Pan, 1/2 Size, 2 1/2" Deep dish evenly spread the sauce mixture. Cover with uncooked lasagna noodles, the cheese mixture, noodles Repeat layers three times. Top with and sauce, Parmesan cheese. Cover with plastic or wax paper and aluminum foil.

4. Bake in a preheated 350 degree F(175 degrees C) oven for 55 minutes. Let stand 20 minutes before serving.

DESSERTS

APPLE TART

Crust

Ingredients:

- 3 cups graham cracker crumbs
- Butter (as needed)

Preparations:

1. Mix crumbs & butter until playable
2. Line baking pan with parchment paper & spray with pan coating
3. Spread crust on paper & bake for 2 minutes at 300°F

Filling

Ingredients:

- 8 apples (Granny Smith)
- 2 tbsp lemon juice
- 3 tbsp flour
- 1 tbsp nutmeg
- 0.5 cup sugar

Preparations:

1. Peel & cut apples, remove seeds
2. Mix all ingredients together
3. Place on crust

Topping

Ingredients:

- ¾ cup flour
- 1 tbsp cinnamon
- ½ cup sugar
- 4 oz butter (cut in cubes)

Preparations:

1. Mix all ingredients by hand in bowl
2. Spread on top of the filling
3. Bake for 40 minutes at 400 F

BANANA BREAD PUDDING

Ingredients:

- 3 lb eggs
- 1.5 lb sugar
- 3 tbsp cinnamon
- 3 lb ripe bananas
- 1 tsp Mace
- 1 tsp nutmeg
- 1 tsp butter
- 1 tsp vanilla
- 8 oz (½ bottle) banana liquor
- 3.5 lb cut bread
- 32 oz Heavy Cream
- 16 oz Water

BANANA PANCAKES

10 lb box pancake mix

Fallow Recipe and Add:

- 1.5 lb sugar
- 3 tbsp baking powder

- 3 lb ripe bananas
- 1 oz butter
- 1 oz vanilla
- 2 oz banana
- ½ bottle banana liquor

BROWNIES

Ingredients:

• 37 eggs

• 6 lb 12 oz sugar

• 4 oz vanilla extract

• 1 pint rum

Directions:

Step 1: Whip together above ingredients until white (10 minutes)

• 5 lb butter

• 4 lb chocolate

Step 2: Melt and mix butter and chocolate until smooth

• 3 lb all purpose flour (sifted)

- 1 lb 4 oz pecans (do not over mix)

- 3 each 2" full hotel pans (buttered and floured)

- 1 lb 8 oz pecans

Step 3: Add flour and first batch of pecans to prior mix. Do not over mix pecans. Once batter is in the pans sprinkle remaining pecans on top of batter. Bake at 350 degrees F for 30 minutes then cover with pan and bake for 10 more minutes.

CARROT CAKE

<u>Ingredients:</u>

- 8 eggs
- 1½ cups butter
- 1 lb 12 oz sugar
- 1 tsp salt
- 1 lb 2 oz bread flour
- 3 tbsp cinnamon
- 1½ tsp baking soda
- ½ tsp baking powder
- 2 lbs shredded carrots
- 5 oz walnuts

Directions:

Step 1: Beat eggs and sugar, then add butter and salt

Step 2: Sift flour; baking soda; and baking powder, then add to eggs mix

Step 3: Then add carrots and walnuts

Step 4: Bake at 375 degrees F for 50 minutes

Filling

Ingredients:

- 28 oz cream cheese
- 2 tsp vanilla
- 1 lb sugar

Directions:

Whip all together.

CHOCOLATE CHIP COOKIES

Ingredients:

- 12 oz brown sugar
- 12 oz granulated sugar
- 18 oz butter
- 4 eggs
- 2 tsp vanilla
- 26 oz bread flour
- 2 tsp salt
- 2 tsp baking soda
- 12 oz chopped walnut
- 24 oz chocolate chips

Directions:

1. In large bowl put brown sugar; granulated sugar and butter
2. Mix with hook until creamy
3. Add eggs one by one
4. Sift together vanilla; bread flour; salt and baking soda then add to mix
5. Mix in last chopped walnuts
6. Divide 4 form ropes and cut. Bake at 350 degrees F until edges are turning brown.

<u>5 times recipe:</u>

- 4 lb sugar
- 4 lb brown sugar
- 5 lb butter
- 3 oz or 20 eggs
- 2 tbsp vanilla
- 4 lb walnuts
- 8 lb 2 oz flour
- 7.5 oz chips
- 10 tsp salt

KEY LIME TART

Makes 3 ½ sheet trays

<u>Ingredients:</u>

- 5 cups granulated sugar
- 24 whole eggs
- 12 egg yolks
- 2 crab cups freshly squeezed lime juice or to taste
- 2 crab cups key lime juice or to taste
- Zest of 4 limes
- 3 lb butter
- ½ qt of heavy cream

- Pinch of salt

Procedure:

1. Combine sugar, eggs, yolks, butter, and half of the lime juices in a stainless steel pot.
2. Cook over medium heat until the mixture starts to thicken (be careful as the eggs can curdle).
3. Once the mixture thickens, immediately strain through a fine mesh strainer.
4. Add in the heavy cream, lime zest, and the remaining lime juices (always check for taste, the tart should be on the tart side).
5. Place the custard on top of the graham cracker crust and bake at 350°F for about 15 minutes or until it is just set and still a little wobbly in the middle.
6. Cool at room temperature, then chill in the refrigerator until very cold.
7. Chill for at least 4 hours before serving.

Graham Cracker Crust:

Ingredients:

- 36 oz graham cracker crumbs
- 20 oz melted butter
- 1 cup sugar

Procedure:

1. Combine all the ingredients and place equal amounts onto 3 ½ sheet trays. Press firmly down with a metal spoon.
2. Garnish with lime whipped cream, raspberry sauce, blackberries and mint.

LEMON TUILE COOKIES

Ingredients:

- 6 egg whites, large not jumbo
- 6 oz flour
- 6 oz powder sugar
- 6 oz melted butter
- 2 lemons, zested on a micro planer
- Pinch of cayenne pepper

Procedure:

1. Sift the flour and powdered sugar together
2. Fold in the butter and egg white
3. Add in the lemon zest and cayenne pepper
4. Heat an oven to 350°F

5. Cook the tuile batter using a Silpat for the best result

6. Spread a thin layer of batter onto the Silpat using any shape mold you want

7. Cook the cookie just until the edges start to turn golden

8. Remove the cookies from the oven and immediately remove them from the sheet tray

9. Mold them into whatever shape you like—for example, drape them over a rolling pin to form a half-moon shape

10. Once the cookies have cooled and their shapes are set, store them in an airtight container

11. The tuiles will keep best in a place with the least amount of humidity

***You can double or triple this recipe when need be.

PASSION FRUIT & MANGO CRÈME BRULEE

Makes 24 6 oz servings

<u>Ingredients:</u>

- 2 tsp vanilla extract or 2 vanilla beans
- 1 ¼ lb or 20 oz. sugar or vanilla sugar

- 1 qt egg yolks
- 3 ½ quarts heavy cream
- 1 tsp salt
- 8 oz passion fruit puree
- Granulated sugar for caramelizing the brulee

Procedure:

1. If using the vanilla bean, cut it lengthwise and scrap the pods out and mix with the sugar (put the stems in sugar to make vanilla sugar). Combine the sugar and egg yolks together and mix well, but do not whip. Heat the cream to the scalding point, and then gradually add into the egg mixture while stirring constantly. Add the salt and the vanilla.

2. Place the diced mango in the bottom of the 3 ¼ inch in diameter oven proof soufflé molds and over with the custard mixture (make sure you fill the molds all the way to the top with the custard mix because they will settle slightly. Place the soufflé molds in a hotel pan before fill with the custard. Add hot water to the hotel pan until the water comes up to ¾ the height of the molds. Bake the custard at 350* for about 25 minutes or until they are set.

3. Do not over bake. Remove the custard from the water bath and allow too cool at room

temperature before chilling in the refrigerator. Chill completely before serving. The custard will last 4 days if covered tightly.

4. Sprinkle just enough sugar on each of the custards to cover the brulee and torch until the custard until it is golden to dark brown, but not brunt.

5. Garnish each brulee with a lemon tuile and fresh raspberries.

PECAN PIES
(Recipe for 10 pies)

Ingredients:

- 10 oz cake flour
- 10 oz granulated sugar
- 15 lb light corn syrup
- 5 lb egg whites
- 4 tbsp vanilla
- 2½ oz salt
- 1 lb melted butter
- 5 oz per pie pecans

Directions:

1. Sift flour, mix with sugar and syrup
2. Whip eggs, add vanilla, then combine with the flour mixture
3. Add butter
4. Place 5 ounces of pecans in shells and pour in the mixture
5. Bake at 325°F until dry

SAUCES & DRESSINGS

BBQ SAUCE

<u>Ingredients:</u>

- 1 No. 10 can ketchup
- 80 oz hot water
- 16 oz white vinegar
- 4 oz balsamic vinegar
- 13 oz hickory smoke
- 2 oz lemon juice
- 4 oz honey
- 2 tbsp (½ oz) dry mustard
- 2 tbsp (½ oz) cumin
- 1 tbsp allspice
- ¼ tbsp cinnamon
- 1 cup (8 oz) dark chili powder
- 1¼ tbsp celery salt
- 1½ tbsp black pepper
- 1 tbsp cayenne pepper
- 1.5 oz sea salt
- 1½ cups (12 oz) brown sugar
- 1 oz poblano pepper
- ½ oz fresh oregano
- ½ oz fresh thyme
- ½ oz fresh basil
- 1.5 oz fresh garlic

Directions:

1. Mix the ingredients in the above order and store in the refrigerator for at least 12 hours
2. Prepare the recipe one or two days before the BBQ for best results
3. You can apply the sauce to meat, chicken, shrimp, or fish before cooking for a stronger flavor
4. You can also apply the sauce after cooking, depending on your preference

BURNT-ORANGE SAUCE
(For the Flan)

Ingredients:

- 28 oz granulated sugar
- 1 cup water
- 2 tsp lemon juice
- 40 oz fresh squeezed orange juice
- Zest of 2 oranges

Procedure:

1. Put the sugar in a heavy-gauge pot and add the water and 1 tablespoon lemon juice.
2. Cook the sugar until a dark caramel, but not burnt.
3. Wash down the sides of the pot frequently with a pastry brush and cold water to stop crystallization of sugar.
4. As soon as the caramel is the right color, add in the orange juice, remaining lemon juice, and zest.
5. Be very careful not to let the caramel splash over the edge because it is extremely dangerous at this point.
6. After the orange juice has been added, the sauce may be reduced to the desired consistency.

COFFEE CRÈME ANGLAISE

Makes 12 cups

Ingredients:

- 24 egg yolks or 2 cups
- 20 oz sugar
- 2 tsp vanilla extract or 2 vanilla beans

- 2 qt ½ & ½
- Coffee extract, to taste

<u>Procedure:</u>

1. Combine the sugar and egg yolks in a mixing bowl and whisk until light and fluffy
2. If using the vanilla bean, scrape the seeds out of the pods and add to the ½ & ½ along with the pods
3. Scald the ½ & ½
4. Gradually pour the hot cream into the yolk mixture while stirring rapidly
5. Put the mixture into a non-reactive pan and cook gently until the mixture coats the back of a spoon
6. As soon as the sauce is ready, add the vanilla and coffee extracts
7. Remove from the heat and immediately strain through a fine mesh strainer and put in a clean container
8. Chill in an ice bath
9. Cover and refrigerate
10. This sauce will last for up to one week as long as it is not disturbed

HONEY RUM SAUCE

Ingredients:

- 6 lb honey
- 8 oz Mayer's rum
- 2 bunches thyme
- 3 cloves garlic
- 3 tsp lemon juice
- 1 lb ginger
- 1 habanero pepper
- 1 tsp mace
- 4 lb water
- ¼ tsp allspice
- 3 sprigs sage
- 2 tbsp chicken base

Directions:

Add bases and spices and simmer for 30 min. and strain.

MANGO SAUCE

Ingredients:

- 3 small red onions
- 3 jalapenos
- 3 anaheins
- 3 poblanos
- 4 peaces of garlic
- ½ cup of red vinegar
- ½ cup of honey
- ½ case of mango chunks
- 3 cans of diced tomatoes
- 1 can of tomatoe juice
- 1 case of fresh mango

Procedure:

1. Heat a pan
2. Cook the onions and peppers
3. Add the vinegar and honey
4. Cook for 3 minutes
5. Add the diced tomatoe and the juice
6. Add the mango chunks and cook for 45 minutes
7. Cool it down then blended
8. Add the frehs mango

RUM CARAMEL SAUCE

Makes 1 ½ quarts

Ingredients:

- 2 lb granulated sugar
- 2/3 cups water
- 1 tsp lemon juice
- 4 tsp light corn syrup
- 3 cups heavy cream
- 2 oz butter
- 1 vanilla bean or vanilla extract or compound
- Myer's dark rum, to taste it should be strong
- 1 cup bitter sweet chocolate

Procedure:

1. Place the sugar, water, and lemon juice in a heavy-gauge non-reactive saucepan
2. Brush down the sides of the pan with water and a pastry brush
3. Add the corn syrup
4. Cook over medium heat until the sugar turns into a dark amber liquid
5. Stand away from the caramel and slowly add in the heavy cream, stirring constantly (be very

careful—the caramel is very hot and dangerous;
do not touch with bare hands)

6. Whisk in the butter, vanilla seeds, chocolate,
and the rum

DOUGH RECIPES

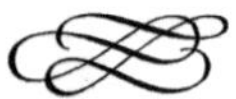

TART DOUGH FOR PINEAPPLE TARTS

Makes 8 lb of dough

Ingredients:

- 24 oz granulated sugar
- 3 lb 8 oz unsalted butter, at room temperature
- 4 eggs
- 2 tsp vanilla extract
- 2 tsp apple cider vinegar
- 4 lb 4 oz all-purpose flour
- 2 tsp salt

Procedure:

1. Place the sugar and butter in the KitchenAid and mix on low speed with the paddle attachment until just incorporated
2. Add in the eggs, vanilla, and apple cider vinegar and mix until incorporated
3. Combine the salt with the flour and gradually add the flour until the dough is smooth
4. Do not overmix in the KitchenAid
5. Place the dough between two sheets of plastic wrap and roll out fairly thin
6. Chill for at least 30 minutes before rolling out the tart shell

7. Once the tart shells are rolled out, prick the bottoms of the shells
8. Bake at 375°F until the dough is golden brown
9. The shells can be frozen at this point to maintain freshness

PART III
FOOD DESCRIPTOR

<u>Freshly Shucked Cherrystone Clams</u>, served raw on the half shell, by the piece. Served with a Lemon wedge and cocktail sauce. These clams are harvested from the Chesapeake Bay and Long Island Sound. Like oysters, they are tagged and FDA approved.

If the guest requests steamed clams, we can accommodate them, but alert them that the cook time is extremely long. Ring in the amount of clams desired and modify with steamed.

The word Cherrystone describes the size of a clam. It can also be called cohog, surf or chowder clam. A guest may ask you for a top neck or little neck. These are the same clams. The difference is the age of the clam and how much it has grown.

<u>Freshly Shucked Oysters</u>, served raw on the half shell, by the piece with a lemon wedge and cocktail sauce. Our oysters are harvested from the Long Island Sound in both Connecticut & New York.

Clams Casino, served with a lemon crown. **Six Whole Cherrystone** clams flavored with spicy butter mix, topped with diced bell peppers and bacon, and baked.

Steamed Mussels, served with a **beurre blanc**, a lemon crown, and a cocktail fork. You will provide the table with a shell bowl. The mussels are from Prince Edward Island in Canada and are rope cultured in FDA approved beds.

Barbecue Scallops Wrapped in Bacon, served on a leaf of lettuce with a lemon crown. **Four jumbo sized** Sea Scallops wrapped with a slice of bacon, partially cooked in a fryer, then flavored with a tangy barbecue sauce and broiled until cooked medium rare. Our scallops are harvested from great beds that lie on the continental shelf from New England to South Carolina. Jumbo means less than 10 scallops to the pound.

Deep Fried Alligator, served with cocktail and tarter sauces, and lemon crown. Tender bite size chunks of alligator meat egg washed and dipped in flour and deep-fried. Alligator meat comes from three areas on the body- the tail, jaw, and body. We use the body tenderloin. FYI! It is legal to harvest alligator only two months out of the year- September & October!

<u>Popcorn Shrimp</u>, served over a leaf of lettuce with cocktail sauce and a lemon crown. It is one half pound of 41/50 count size shrimp dipped in egg wash, Old Bay, and breadcrumbs, then deep fried. They are breaded fresh to order.

FYI!!! The range of the catch is from under 10 per pound to 150/200 per pound!

<u>Shrimp Cocktail</u>, served in a bowl on a leaf of lettuce over crushed ice, with cocktail sauce and a lemon crown. **Four colossal** shrimp, 10-12 per pound, steamed fresh daily. Our shrimp are domestic, from the Gulf of Mexico. Guests will often ask for Tiger shrimp, which is a farm-raised product that does not compare in flavor to wild caught.

<u>Deep Fried Calamari</u> served with marinara sauce and a lemon crown. 5-8 inch size squid made up of both tentacles and tubes. It is egg washed and dipped in flour, then deep- fried to a golden brown. A very popular starter.

<u>Smoked Pastrami Salmon Plate</u>, Cold smoked salmon marinated in pastrami spices, served with capers, red onions, hard-boiled egg, tomatoes, cream cheese, and crackers. This product is available from Ocean Pro.

<u>T&J's Homemade Shoestring Onion Rings</u>, a very generous portion served in a large bowl. Very thinly sliced.

Fried Catfish Fingers, served with tarter sauce. Eight ounces of farm raised catfish, dipped in egg and breadcrumbs and fried to golden brown.

Chicken Tenders, served with barbecue sauce and honey mustard sauce. Eight ounces of chicken tenders approximately one ounce each dipped in egg wash, coated with breadcrumbs, then fried.

Hot Crab Dip, served with garlic toast croutons and lemon crown. A blend of claw and backfin crabmeat with cream, garlic, and Parmesan cheese mixed together, topped with breadcrumbs, and baked.

Smoked Salmon, Artichoke & Spinach Dip, served with garlic toast croutons. Parmesan, provolone, and cream cheese, pieces of smoked salmon, artichoke, and spinach leaves blended together and baked. Note: the smoked salmon is blended in the dip, not on the side!

Crabmeat Appetizer, Jumbo lump crabmeat served cold w/ cocktail sauce.

Steamed Spiced Shrimp, served with Old Bay mixed with white vinegar and a lemon. One dozen 16/20 size shrimp, steamed to order. Can be messy.

HOMEMADE SOUPS

All soups are made either daily or every other day. The ingredients are fresh and no preservatives are added. Every one is a great seller.

The serving size is 8 ounces. Served with oyster crackers.

Maryland Crab Soup, Tomato based, made from crab stock. Includes: Tomatoes, corn, onion, green beans, carrots, celery, lima beans, and fresh crabmeat. It is spiced with Old Bay and can be quite hot to a mild palate!

New England Clam Chowder, Traditional style, cream based. Includes: Large potato cubes, onions, celery, **bacon** and chopped clams. Please be aware of certain cultures' dietary concerns in regards to bacon, as many will not assume it to be an ingredient!

<u>Cream of Crab</u>, a velvety cream base. Includes: Corn kernels, and topped with fresh Jumbo Lump Crabmeat. It is more expensive because the ingredients are more expensive. Offer sherry when serving to cut the heaviness.

All dressings are made in the house except Raspberry Low Calorie. All dressings come on the side except for the Dinner salad.

The salad base mix used in all of our salads consists of the following lettuces:

Iceberg, Radicchio, aragulla, watercress, Boston lettuce, and green leaf. Due to availability, the mix may change.

The Dressings...

- **Creamy Dijon Vinaigrette**: Our "house" dressing, made with mayonnaise, red wine vinegar, black pepper, garlic, onion powder, and flavored with Dijon mustard.
- **Caesar**: Anchovies, mayonnaise, egg, olive oil,

red wine vinegar, black pepper, garlic., and parmesan.**(Cannot be ordered w/out cheese)**
- **Herb Vinaigrette**: Olive oil, red wine vinegar, basil, oregano, tarragon, shallots, sugar, salt & pepper.
- **Bleu Cheese**: Sour cream, mayonnaise, white pepper and real Roquefort bleu cheese crumbles.
- **Ranch**: Eggs, olive oil, vinegar, chives, buttermilk, carrots, garlic and onion powder.
- **Raspberry Low Calorie**: Raspberry vinegar, olive oil, sugar, salt, basil and oregano. The low cal comes from a process that removes calories from the olive oil.
- **Caesar Style** (will be made w/ romaine lettuce and tossed with caesar dressing).

Green Dinner Salad, lettuce mix, tomatoes, cucumbers, croutons. Dressing will come on top unless modified "on the side".

Garden House Salad, Romaine and iceberg lettuce, with tomato, cucumber, carrot, Bermuda onions and croutons. This is a slightly larger salad than the Dinner salad.

Tony & Joe's House, lettuce mix, tomatoes, egg, hearts of palm, artichokes and croutons.Variations-

Smoked peppered chicken breast, 4 ounces boneless

breast, flavored in house with liquid smoke and cracked black pepper, served warm.

Grilled Marinated Salmon 4 ounces.

Grilled Tenderloin Salad, Boston lettuce, Bermuda onions, cucumber, egg, and sliced beef tenderloin marinated in BBQ sauce and Jim Beam Bourbon. The steak is cooked medium rare. **Tony & Joe's Caeser**, Romaine lettuce, Parmesan cheese, croutons, tossed in our homemade Caesar dressing.

Availible with Chicken or Smoked Salmon (4oz)as described above

Grilled Scallop Salad, lettuce mix, jumbo size scallops (<10 per pound), tomatoes, pimentos, artichokes, croutons, toasted almonds and 1 butterflied 16/20 shrimp. The sea scallops are lightly grilled and cooked to medium rare.

COLD SANDWICHES

The **Creamed Cucumbers** are a secret family recipe, seasoned with cream, lemon juice, garlic, and dill.

The **Potato Salad** is made from red bliss potatoes, mayo, salt, pepper, and chives.

All of our side salads are made fresh daily on the premises.

<u>Tuna Salad,</u> served on a poppy seed kaiser roll with lettuce and tomato, side of potato salad and creamed cukes. **Albacore white tuna** meat in water tossed with mayo,carrots, pepper and celery.

<u>Shrimp Salad</u>, served on a poppy seed kaiser roll with potato salad and creamed cucumbers. These are **whole shrimp** (41/50per pound) tossed with mayo, celery, and red peppers and chutney.

HOT SANDWICHES

All hot sandwiches are served with curlicue french fries and coleslaw. The coleslaw is made fresh every day from green cabbage, mayo, red wine vinegar, garlic, salt and pepper.

Crabcake Sandwich, served on a poppy seed kaiser roll with lettuce, tomato, and a pickle, and with tarter sauce. A 4-ounce cake, broiled, made entirely of jumbo lump crabmeat with *very* little filler. This is our best selling sandwich!!

Deep Fried Fillet of Fish, served on a sesame seed kaiser roll with lettuce, tomato, pickle and tarter sauce. 5-ounce flounder fillet dipped in egg wash and battered with bread crumbs, then deep fried to golden brown.

King Clip, served on a sesame seed kaiser roll with lettuce, tomato and a pickle, and **tarragon shrimp**

mayonnaise. A 5-ounce piece of King Clip, sauteed and topped with two strips of bacon.

Tuna Steak Burger, served on a sesame seed kaiser roll with lettuce, tomato, a pickle and **pesto mayonnaise**. A 5-ounce tuna steak grilled to customer order.

Shrimp Burger, 6oz of domestic gulf shrimp ground into tender pieces and bound with fresh breadcrumbs. An excellent alternative to the traditional burger, the shrimp burger is full of high energy protein and low in fat!

Fried Oyster, served on a sesame seed kaiser roll with lettuce, tomato, pickle and tarter sauce. Our **oysters**, freshly shucked, egg washed and breaded, then deep fried and topped with bacon.

Chargrilled Hamburger, served on a sesame seed kaiser roll with lettuce, tomato and a pickle. 8-ounces of prime 80/20 lean USDA hamburger cooked to order.

Cheeseburger will come with **cheddar** unless otherwise modified with provolone.

Philadelphia Cheesesteak, served on a sub roll. A very large sandwich made from real strips of NY Strip steak, sautéed with green peppers, mushrooms, and onions and topped with melted provolone cheese.

Chicken Philly is the same sandwich with tender strips of chicken breast.

<u>Chargrilled Breast of Chicken</u>, served on sesame seed kaiser roll with lettuce, tomato and a pickle.

A 6-ounce boneless & skinless breast of chicken topped with melted provolone cheese.

<u>Softshell</u>, served on a seeded kaiser roll with a lemon crown. One crab, egg washed and breaded then deep fried. See entrees.

ENTREES

Unless otherwise noted on the menu (ex. Garlic & Lemon Sea Scallops), entrees will have a choice of starch: Baked Potato, French Fries (dinner fries are steak, not curlicue), Rice, or Linguini. Be sure to ask each guest which side they would prefer whenever applicable. The computer will prompt you to enter their selection, with the exception of Specials, which will come with a baked potato unless modified. The vegetables are A La Carte, and must be verbally sold as "vegetable of the day".

<u>Maryland Style Crabcakes</u>, served with tarter sauce and a lemon crown. Two 4-ounce cakes, broiled, made entirely of jumbo lump crabmeat with *very* little filler.

This is our best selling item for good reason. All of our crabmeat is <u>hand</u> picked. Jumbo lump is the premier of crabmeat. It comes from the Blue Crab, found from the Chesapeake down to the Gulf of Mexico. Maryland Crabs are best because they are fresher and are steamed, not boiled.

Maryland Blue Crabs are usually available from May to November. Although we will not sell hard shell crabs in our restaurant, The Dancing Crab in Tenly Town serves them year round. FYI: we own the Dancing Crab!!!

Dover Sole, from England, served sauteed, the only fish we fillet tableside.

Stuffed Salmon Steak, served with a baked potato. Stuffed and baked with cream spinach, smoked salmon and artichokes.

Seafood Stew, served with garlic croutons and a lemon crown. A tomato spice based bouillabaisse with saffron, full of mussels, clams, shrimp, scallops and fresh fish. The seafood is in the shell, so please provide your table with a shell bowl.

Stuffed and Baked Shrimp, served with a lemon crown and cocktail sauce. Four jumbo shrimp, butterflied, stuffed with a mixture of spinach and cream, jumbo lump crabmeat, cayenne and anisette, and baked.

Grilled Shrimp, served with a lemon crown and linguini with marinara sauce. Five jumbo shrimp, butterflied, skewered, coated with basil garlic butter, and grilled.

Blackened Shrimp, served with a lemon crown. Four jumbo shrimp, butterflied, skewered, dipped in butter, and coated with our own spicy blackening spice, then seared in a cast iron skillet.

Fried Shrimp, served with a lemon crown and cocktail sauce. Four jumbo shrimp, butterflied, egg washed and deep fried.

Garlic and Lemon Sea Scallops, served with a lemon crown over a bed of linguini. 20/30 count scallops sautéed in basil, garlic butter and wine.

T&J's Marinated & Broiled Seafood Platter, served with tarter and cocktail sauce and a lemon crown. Three jumbo shrimp, six scallops, a piece of tilapia fillet, and one crabcake (4 oz).

Stuffed and Baked Flounder, served with a lemon crown. 8 ounces of haddock stuffed with large pieces of shrimp, crabmeat and parsley.

Softshell Crabs, served with a lemon crown. A seasonal dish served only when fresh, they are cleaned of inedible parts, such as face, lungs and tail, and sautéed in white wine, butter and garlic.

FYI: Softshells are blue crabs that have outgrown and

shed their shells, called molting. The crabs will molt about 5 times a year!!!

<u>Sautéed Chicken Breast</u>, sautéed in olive oil and white wine, with mushrooms, scallions and Parmesan cheese.

<u>Stuffed & Baked Chicken Florentine</u>, a 6-ounce filet stuffed with a mixture of spinach, cream, Parmesan cheese, worchestshire sauce and Tabasco and topped with hollandaise sauce.

<u>New York Strip Steak</u>, 12-ounces of Prime aged NY strip hand trimmed for fat and cooked to specification. Topped with a Portobello mushroom and red wine sauce.

<u>Filet Mignon</u>, 12-ounces of Choice cut, served with hollandaise **or** béarnaise sauce.

<u>Rack of Ribs</u>, a full rack of short pork ribs, marinated in barbecue sauce, ketchup, liquid smoke, brown sugar, nutmeg and all spice, grilled and topped with fresh barbecue sauce.

<u>Clams or Mussels Linguini</u>, served over a bed of linguini in a large bowl, you will supply the guest with a shell bowl and offer Parmesan cheese. This is 6 steamed Cherrystone clams or 20 or so mussels. The red sauce is marinara sauce spiced with white clam sauce. The white sauce is clam juice, white wine, chopped clams, red pepper flakes, thyme, oregano, salt and pepper.

<u>Alaskan King Crab Legs</u>, served with a lemon crown, drawn butter, lobster crackers and a cocktail fork, you will supply the guest with a shell bowl and bib. A one pound portion, the price reflects the fact the king crab is hard to acquire. FYI: Fishing king crab is a very dangerous industry. The season is short and the seas are rough and every year a few fishermen are lost at sea who are trying to fish the lucrative King crab!!!

<u>Whole Steamed Maine Lobster</u>, served with a lemon crown, lobster cracker, cocktail fork and melted butter. You will supply the guest with a bib and shell bowl. We will always have lobsters available from 1 ¼ to 2 ½ pounds, sometimes larger.

FRESH FISH

The Steaks...

Tuna - Big Eye and it's flown in from Ecuador. Dark and rich. Cooked medium rare to maximize flavor. Best grilled.

Swordfish- Flown in from Hawaii. Should be plump and juicy, if it's dry, it's overcooked. Best grilled or blackened.

Salmon Steak- Pink, distinctive flavor, mild and firm. Best baked.

The Fillets...

Salmon- Flown in from Canada. Very distinct flavor. Best broiled or steamed.

<u>Mahi- Mahi</u>- Flown in from Costa Rica. Darker than sword, sweet in flavor, light, excellent blackened, grilled.

<u>Halibut</u>-Flown in from Alaska. Large flakes, firm in texture, pure white color. Best broiled, baked, grilled.

<u>Flounder</u>- Caught off the shores of George's Bank in Nova Scotia and North Carolina. Mild flavored, tender flaky texture. Best panfried or broiled.

<u>Dover Sole</u>- From Dover, England, similar to flounder, flat fish, must be filleted at the table b/c of delicateness of the meat. Best sautéed.

Some Others...

<u>Rainbow Trout</u>- Served with tail on, mild taste, soft flesh, best sautéed or pan fried, too delicate to grill.

<u>Red Snapper</u>- Flown in from the Gulf of Mexico. It's a True American Red. Bright red in color, little fat therefore is delicate, and not very distinctive in flavor._Skin on, oily, not too fishy. Best grilled or blackened.

<u>Mako Shark</u>- Tough, like Swordfish, but not as flavorful. Best broiled.

<u>Tilapia</u>- Fresh water, indigenous of South Africa, it is now farm raised in the States. Relative of the Red Snapper, mild in taste, flaky. Best broiled.

<u>Grouper</u>- A deep-water fish, firm texture, white, mild, meaty, slightly fishy. Best grilled.

<u>Rockfish</u>- Indigenous to the area, oily, similar to Red Snapper. Best broiled.

<u>Ocean Perch</u>- Similar to Rockfish, mild and delicate. Firm, white flesh, fishy flavor. Best broiled.

<u>Sea Bass</u>-White moist and flaky with an oily texture, best broiled or baked.

<u>Escolor</u>-Similar to Swordfish, sweeter.

<u>King Clip</u>-From Chile, tastes like a cross between Halibut & Mahi-mahi. Best sauteed.

SAUCES AND BUTTERS

Sauces and Butters

Cocktail sauce- ketchup, horseradish, Worcestershire, Tabasco. Found on the condiment trays in the dining room along with mayonnaise, horseradish, sour cream and tartar.

Tartar sauce- mayonnaise, green olives, capers, lemon juice.

Beurre Blanc- butter, white wine, lemon juice, parsley, garlic.

Marinara sauce- homemade recipe. Tomato base spiced with onions, basil, garlic, pepper.

Barbecue sauce-secret homemade recipe!

Honey mustard- cream, honey, mustard.

Tarragon shrimp mayo- tarragon, shrimp, mayo, dash of cayenne.

Pesto mayo- garlic, basil, walnuts, olive oil, mayonnaise.

Hollandaise- egg yolks, butter, wine, salt, pepper.

Bearnaise- hollandaise sauce with tarragon.

Mustard Dill butter- dill, dijon mustard, salt, butter

Basil Garlic butter- basil leaf, garlic, butter, lemon juice.

Cajun Spice butter- cayenne, salt, pepper, beer, Worcheshire, lemon juice, thyme, oregano, butter.